I love reading

Fantastic Fossils

by Leonie Bennett

Consultant: Dougal Dixon

ticktock

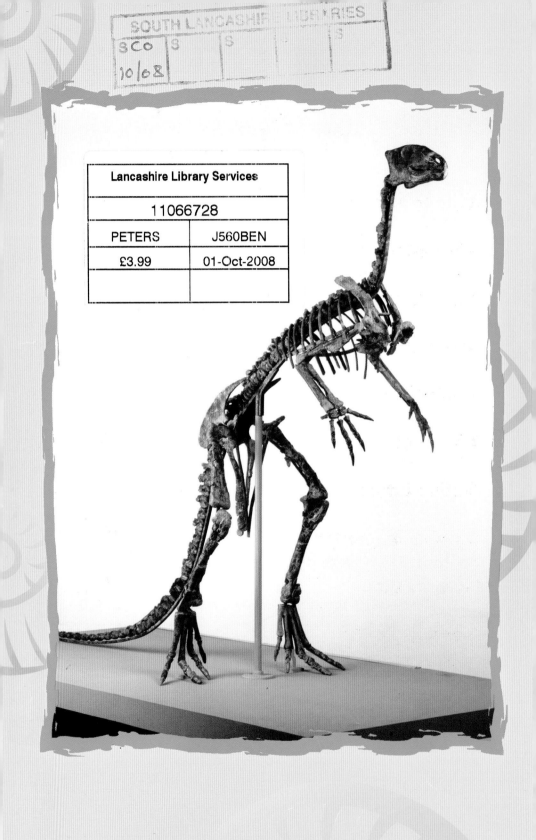

CONTENTS

Words in **bold** are explained in the glossary.

What is a fossil?

Can you see a **dinosaur's** head in this stone?

Fossil

The dinosaur lived long ago. Its bones and teeth have turned into stone!

We call these **fossils**.

The dinosaur might have looked like this.

Different fossils

We can find fossils of footprints.

We can find fossils of plants.

We can find fossils of animals.

Why are fossils important?

We learn a lot from fossils.

We learn about animals
that died long ago.

Look at this fossil.

Can you see the animal's neck?

Can you see the animal's head?

How a dinosaur became a fossil

Look at **Hypsilophodon**.
It lived millions of years ago.

It fell into a lake and died.

Hypsilophodon
hip-sil-o-fo-don

11

At the bottom of a lake

It fell to the bottom of the lake.
Other animals ate its skin.

Its bones lay on the bottom of the lake.

Bones

A fossil at last

Mud and sand covered the bones.

Millions of years went by.

The bones turned into stone.

Mud and sand

The dinosaur was now a fossil.

It lay in the rock for a long time.

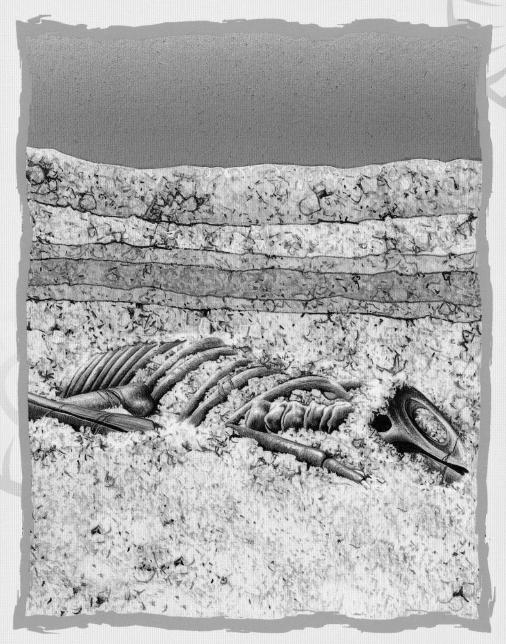

Finding a fossil

Over time, the ground moved.

A girl saw a fossil in some rock.

She told some **scientists**.

The scientists came to dig up the fossils.

It's Hypsilophodon!

The scientists worked out what the dinosaur looked like.

They put the fossils of the dinosaur
in a museum.

More fossils

Tyrannosaurus rex
tie-ran-o-sor-us rex

T. rex was a fierce hunter.

Ichthyosaur
ik-thee-o-sor

Ichthyosaur means 'fish-lizard'.

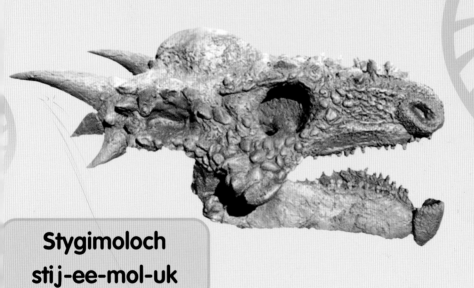

Stygimoloch
stij-ee-mol-uk

This dinosaur is also called
a bonehead.

Glossary

dinosaur
A lizard-like animal that lived millions of years ago.

fossil
A part of an animal or plant that has turned into stone. Footprints can also be fossils.

Hypsilophodon
A small dinosaur that ate plants.

scientist
A person who is an expert in science.

Index

Copyright © ticktock Entertainment Ltd 2008
First published in Great Britain in 2008 by ticktock Media Ltd.,
Unit 2, Orchard Business Centre, North Farm Road, Tunbridge Wells, Kent TN2 3XF
ISBN 978 1 84696 756 6 pbk
Printed in China

We would like to thank: Penny Worms, Shirley Bickler, Suzanne Baker and the National Literacy Trust.

Picture credits (t=top, b=bottom, c=centre, l-left, r=right, OFC= outside front cover)
Corbis: 17, 18, 23b; Ian Jackson: 1, 10, 11, 12, 13, 14, 15, 23t; Simon Mendez: 5; Natural History Museum: 19, 21t; Shutterstock: 4, 6-7, 16, 20, 22t, 22b; ticktock Media Archive: 1, 8-9, 21b.

Every effort has been made to trace the copyright holders, and we apologise in advance for any unintentional omissions. We would be pleased to insert the appropriate acknowledgements in any subsequent edition of this publication.